55 Fun Things To Do With Your Baby

Age Appropriate Activities For Parents And Children

Christie Cunningham

Dedication

For Elijah.

55 Fun Things To Do With Your Baby

Age Appropriate Activities For Parents And Children

Table of Contents

Introduction

The door closed softly as my husband left for work for the first time since our son was born. There we were, staring into each others' eyes as if we were both saying to the other, "Now what?"

"Are you going to cry?" I asked him.

"Are *you*?" He seemed to respond, wordlessly.

Fair enough. If you find yourself alone with a baby of any age, but especially babies under one year of age, for the first time – those who cannot speak, cannot walk, perhaps cannot crawl, sit up, roll, or even hold their own heads up – you may quickly find yourself wondering "Now what?" just as I was.

For those of us who are just recently out of the working world, or who are at the very least used to some adult conversation every now and then, finding ourselves face to face with a little guy or gal who *needs* us 24/7/365 can be extremely challenging. And as all new parents know, babies don't come with instruction manuals (just tons and tons of advice from well-meaning friends, family, and strangers).

What we do know is that there are countless studies that tell us the BEST things we can do with our babies: love them, hold them, and TALK to them. Talking to babies (a lot) has been shown to actually increase their IQ![1] Although all babies need some alone time every now and then, they otherwise LOVE being showered with attention from their mamas and papas.

Some important tips on baby play and toys:

- Babies need quiet time too. You'll know your little guy or gal needs a break if he or she is fussing and looking away from you. If so, give him or her a moment to regroup and rest without trying to make eye contact. When your baby turns his or her head back to you, you'll know it's time to play again!
- Never give your baby anything to play with that is small enough to fit through a toilet paper tube (e.g. marbles, spools of thread, balloons, which can deflate and become this size, or toys with parts that can detach and would be this small). These items are also small enough to fit down your baby's throat and can be a severe choking hazard.
- Babies are fragile! Make sure any activity you engage in with your child is appropriate for his or her growth and strength. Always check with your doctor.

---

[1] If you want to know more about this and ways to increase your baby's IQ, check out "Brain Rules for Baby" by John Medina.

- Baby carriers and strollers vary greatly. If you plan to walk or jog with your baby in a carrier or stroller, make sure he or she is old enough and strong enough for the type of activity you plan to engage in. Read the carrier/stroller's directions carefully.

I hope these activities will provide great motivation for you and your spouse to stay engaged with your child by providing suggestions and mutually beneficial ideas for interactions.

Chapter 1:
Activities For
Especially Young
Babies

While your baby is very new he or she will spend most of the day eating, sleeping, crying, or dirtying a diaper. However, every once in a while there will be a time (often called "quiet alert time") when your baby is ready to engage with you and be entertained. When you find one of these moments, try out a few of our suggested activities for especially young babies (about 0 to 3 months old):

1. Making Faces

Although we often don't encourage older kids to make faces, it's really fun to do with babies. Some studies have shown that babies can mimic our facial expressions in less than an hour after they are born.[2] Try sticking out your tongue at your baby (hold it out for a

---

[2] Again, see "Brain Rules for Baby" by John Medina.

bit so your baby can study it) and see if he or she replicates. You can also make a big "O" out of your mouth and see if you get a similar response back from that. You probably won't get a smile back until your child is at least two months old, or probably older.

2. Kangaroo Care

One of the best things you can do with a newborn is to get that precious skin-to-skin time (critical for mothers *and* fathers). Strip your baby's clothes off (you can leave diaper on if you'd like) and place him or her directly on your chest without any material in between. (You can keep a large sweatshirt on if you or baby will get cold – just have your baby inside your shirt with his or her little head peeking out the neck hole with yours.) Your baby will love the softness of your skin, getting to know your smell, and the tenderness of the interaction.

3. Dance To Your Favorite Song

Putting on your favorite music (not too loud, of course) and getting up and dancing is not only fun for your baby, but for you too! Your baby will love being held close to you (be careful to fully support baby's head and neck) as you gently dance together, and this activity may even help to calm a fussy baby. See if you and your baby can find a new favorite song together! (Hint: For whatever reason, fussy babies often like the beat of reggae music. Go figure! Try a little Bob Marley and see how it works for you.)

4. Baby Concert

You can modify the above activity by letting your baby lie down on a safe surface (like buckled into his or her swing), or lying in a Moses basket on the floor) while you dance for his or her enjoyment. The better the show you put on, the better the response you'll get. If the reviews are lackluster, try shaking your booty or getting those jazz hands and spirit fingers going.

5. Test Baby's Senses

When baby's are first born their vision is very poor, but it improves quickly with time. Newborns can generally only see things (or focus on things) about 12 – 15 inches from their faces, so if you're playing games where you want him or her to see something, try to keep the distance about a foot away or a bit more. It can be fun as baby gets older to test how his or her vision is improving. To do this, get a rattle or one of baby's favorite toys to shake to the left or right and see if baby turns to look (hearing) and fixes his or her gaze on the object (sight). It may be difficult at first, but over time that distance will grow and soon your baby will be tracking your movement from across the room!

6. Read A Book

You may have an extensive collection of books just waiting to be read to your baby. Well, even though Baby isn't old enough to fully appreciate the storyline of your favorite book (or even "Goodnight, Moon") it doesn't mean he or she won't enjoy hearing you read, seeing your eye contact, and looking at the high contrast images. For a change of pace, you can even read your favorite magazine or the sports scores to your baby!

7. Explore Your World

Your baby will love being your sidekick as you take him or her around to explore. Try a different room in your house each day. Talk to baby about the tiniest details in each room and you'll be amazed how much time you might spend! For example, you can talk about the way a window is framed, the type of glass used, whether it's double pane, the size of the nails used, what kinds of blinds or curtains you have, their texture and color…and all that is just about a window! Imagine how long it will take you to get through the kitchen! As you go, let your baby feel each object (if it's safe) that you mention. Feel the fabric, feel the coolness of the glass, and feel the smooth wood, all while you describe it. You'll get bonus points for showing objects that make a fun noise.

8. Dress Up

Your baby has a limited number of items he or she can wear right now, but will learn to love watching you get dressed in a variety of ridiculous outfits. Almost anything can be a hat (pots, pans, Tupperware, pillows), jackets can be put on backwards and upside down, just think outside the box! As you go putting on one ridiculous thing after the other, let your baby feel the different fabrics you're getting out: from knitted scarves, to silk dresses, to cotton socks balled up.

9. Photo Shoot

Tiny, new babies make the best photo shoot subjects. Turn up the heat in your house so your little one will be comfortable (if you can go as high as 85 degrees, you'll be all set), or pick a particularly warm day for this activity if your baby is a summer baby and you won't need to pay for heating at all. Take your babies clothes (and diaper!) off and set him or her up on a soft blanket, in a safe place (like the floor) where baby won't roll off and go anywhere. Get out your best camera and set the aperture to the smallest number you can (like f-1.2) so you'll have a nice shallow depth of field. Use natural light if you can to get the best shot possible. Take lots of pictures so you can choose from a variety. Set your baby up in your spouse's hands, hold his or her tiny feet in your hands, or show a close up of his or her hands holding your finger. These also make great announcement cards or gifts for relatives!

10. Magic Wand

While your baby is quite young, you'll have to be the only sorcerer or sorceress in the house for a while, as it will be a few more months until your little one can hold his or her own magic wand. However, you can fill the role well by making a spectacular wand for yourself (think about fun things like yarn or a scarf tied securely around a wooden spoon) and wave it around in the air above your baby while he or she watches.[3] You can

---

[3] Make sure to disassemble this and secure any loose strings or fabric that might get near your baby once you're done playing to avoid the risk of strangulation.

practice your best spells (like for a diaper that changes itself).

11. See-Through Peek-A-Boo

Young babies don't yet have the skill known as "Object Permanence." That means that once an object is out of the babies view, he or she believes that it ceases to exist. You can have some real fun with peek-a-boo as your baby gets older, but when he or she is very young, you can start with a watered down version by holding an object in front of your face that is translucent and talking to your baby through it. Try thin scarves, clear Tupperware, or other objects that partially obscure you from view.

12. Engage In Interactive Songs

There are a myriad of interactive songs you can try out to find your baby's favorite. For example, try "The Itsy Bitsy Spider" (though it will be a while before baby can do this along with you), "Patty Cake" (we always substitute the first letter of his name for B when marking the cake), "The Wheels on the Bus," "Old MacDonald Had A Farm," "Bingo Was His Name-O," "Row, Row, Row Your Boat."

13. Invest In A Gymini

Although I don't advocate buying your child a bunch of toys (especially because he or she will generally prefer the box to the toy) one of the toys we got the absolute MOST use out of for our baby was a gymini – basically, a play mat (often jungle themed) with arms that stretch across above it and have toys that dangle down. Your baby can lie on his back and learn to swing at the hanging animals, and can enjoy tummy time by looking at the colorful designs beneath him or her. Our baby played on his Gymini multiple times a day and didn't tire of it for *months*!

14. Discuss The Family Tree

Babies love to look at faces, especially faces they know (like yours)! Get out a photo album or even a stack of photos (if you're one of those parents – like me! – who just hasn't had time to get to working on your photo album lately) and hold them up one at a time about 12-16 inches from your baby's face. As your baby studies the faces in the photo, tell him or her about the person in the photo. Your baby will come to see these faces as familiar and safe, and will love to hear your voice talking sweetly as he or she learns.

15. Tummy Time!

Tummy time is a crucial part of helping your baby to improve his or her neck strength. Back when babies slept on their tummies (that was the "safe" thing to do back in the day, now it's BACK ONLY for sleep!) they were able to hold their heads up much sooner on average. Now that babies sleep exclusively on their backs, we must make sure they get some time on their tummies each day to play and get strong. You can make this more fun by getting down on the floor to play. If the baby fusses right away about being face down, just let him or her play for 30 to 60 seconds, pick baby up, and try again later.

Although we start with tummy time in this section for new babies this activity, and many others listed in this chapter, are great as your baby gets older too.

Chapter 2:
Indoor Activities

Depending on when your son or daughter is born and where you live, you may be spending some long stretches of the year inside due to rain, snow, or freezing temperatures. If that's the case for you, try out a few of these fun indoor activities:

16. Invest in an ExerSaucer

Although I'm a big fan of not having to buy a lot of things to entertain one's baby, I just mentioned the Gymini, which is a great product, and the only other "toy" I'll really recommend is an ExerSaucer.[4] This contraption is sort of like a 360 degree play station for your child. Fabric helps him or her to "stand" (while not straining joints) and "jump" and can generally be used as soon as your baby can support his neck. It has lots of fun stations for your baby to swivel between and enjoy new sensations, sounds, and experiences.

17. Play "Rear Window"

The world outside is an exciting place – even when you're trapped indoors. Take time with your baby to

---

[4] You need not buy either of these new. Most baby consignment stores have PLENTY in their inventory!

look outside each day and talk about what you see. From the weather to the comings and goings of your neighbors, there's always a lot to learn, see, and experience.

18. Play "Facial Expressions" In The Mirror

We already discussed how much your baby will love to watch your facial expressions change, and maybe even mirror them, but this gets taken up another fun notch as your child gets several months older and can watch him or herself (and you) in the mirror and see what fun that mommy or daddy and baby are having.

19. Hit The Gym (Baby Sit Ups)

When your baby is first born, he or she is too young for pony rides and other more vigorous games. When that muscle strength, and neck strength are ready (check with doctor), you can start to play games with your baby while he or she is sitting up. One of these involves seeing your little one perform gentle feats of strength. While you're seated, let your baby lie on his back on your legs. While holding onto your baby's hands, slightly extended from his body, see if he starts to pull on your hands. If so, keep them where they are, and your little guy or gal may start pulling up into a mini sit up. Don't pull on your baby's arms or pull him up if his neck is loose. Let him guide you.

20. Give "Pony Rides"

I still remember getting pony rides (though I was older) from my Dad. Once your baby's neck strength is well established, this is a fun game. Just place your baby on your knee and hold onto him or her around the middle while bouncing him or her up and down and singing:

(Very gentle, low bounce) "This is the way the lady rides, lady rides, lady rides. This is the way the lady rides so early in the morning."

(Slightly more vigorous bounce, slightly higher) "This is the way the gentleman rides, gentleman rides, gentleman rides. This is the way the gentleman rides so early in the morning."

(Most vigorous – but not too hard – and highest bounce. Make sure you're supporting your baby well.) "This is the way the farmer rides, farmer rides, farmer rides. This is the way the farmer rides so early in the morning."

21. Jack in the Box or Pop Goes the Weasel (surprise games)

Some babies, depending on temperament, really enjoy little, fun surprises. If you think your baby would be up for it, you can try out this little game by singing the song while making some fun hand gestures to go along. ("All around the mulberry bush the monkey chased the weasel. The monkey thought 'twas all in fun – POP – goes the weasel.") Once you get to the POP, do something surprising. You can start with making a face and work your way up to more and more surprising things like adding in a clap (softly at first, and a little louder if it goes over well). Your baby will learn to anticipate the surprise is coming (fun in itself to see), and will delight to see what new things you'll do next.

22. Cook Together

Over the course of your baby's first year of life, you will inevitably be doing some cooking. Instead of just finding a place to put your baby down to entertain his or herself for the entire time you're busy, see if you can incorporate baby into the tasks. Sit him or her up in a high chair where baby won't be able to reach anything dangerous (the stove, pot handles, knives, etc.) and then talk about what you're doing. You can let him or her play with the measuring spoons, bowls, or spatulas, and maybe even sneak a small piece of chopped up vegetable once he or she is eating (make sure it's the right size and not a choking hazard)!

23. Play Hide and Seek

Although your baby isn't old enough to go tearing through the house to find you, that doesn't mean he or she isn't interested in the mystery and excitement of a hunt. During tummy time or play time on a mat you can hide little toys and favorite objects under scarves, Tupperware, cups, and the like for your baby to hunt for and discover.

24. Play Peek-A-Boo

This is another game that leverages the element of surprise. You'll find as your baby gets closer to 6 months old that he or she loves to see you pop around a corner or see your face come up over the edge of a book to peer at him or her. This is a fun game to play any time. Just hide around a corner and pop out with a smile, catching your baby's eye. You can amp up the anticipation by talking to your baby while you're out of sight, "Where's Daddy?" or "Where's Mommy?" and then pop into view – "Peek-a-boo!" You can also play the simpler version, just sitting with your baby on your lap and hiding your face in your hands.

25. Baby Reads A Book

We already talked about reading books to your baby as soon as he or she is born. Even though babies can't understand or follow a plot, getting into the habit of reading together will be great for both of you. That said, as your baby gets older, he or she *will* be able to interact with books much more, focusing on high contrast images, feeling texture books, and even turning pages. At this older age, take the time to let your baby be the one to hold the book and interact with different things on the page. If your baby seems done with a page (even if you're still reading it), just let him or her turn the page and move on. This will help keep baby engaged and entertained.

26. Sing "Head, Shoulders, Knees, and Toes"

One of the first "games" I played with my baby was the "Head, Shoulders, Knees, and Toes" game/song. While I sang those body parts over and over, I gently touched those parts of my baby. As he grew, I was then able to amp things up by holding his hands while I sang and moving *his* hands to touch his head, shoulders, knees, and toes (he especially loves grabbing at his tiny toes). When he's older, he'll graduate to doing these motions on his own while learning about the different parts of his body.

27. Diffuse The Missile

This game is brought to us by my father-in-law by way of my husband. With the baby lying on his back on our lap, we launch little "missiles" at him (a hand with the fingers all together, heading at the baby fingers first) while making a whistling sound. He has to try to touch each missile before it gets to his body. If he does, the missile "explodes" in mid-air with a great explosion sound. If not, the missile lands on him, giving him lots of tickles as it "explodes." You can increase the level of difficulty by sending out multiple missiles at once (using both hands) and increasing the speed of the missiles. Very fun!

28. Make Faces In The Mirror

It will be a long time before your baby will be able to recognize/ understand that he's looking at *himself* in the mirror, but in the meantime, he sure doesn't mind checking out that cute baby his mommy or daddy is holding! Holding your baby's face up close to yours, bring him or her closer and farther from the mirror, making smiling faces, surprised faces, and other silly looks and your little one is likely to match your expression and crack up in the process!

29. Give A Bath

Once your baby outgrows his or her baby bath you may be ready to start giving baths in the full size tub. If that's the case and your baby isn't ready to sit up alone yet, spending some time in the tub with your little one can be a fun way to pass some time. After you've gotten the temperature just right and set out a towel, change of diaper, and fresh clothes, get some other fun items ready. It is **very important** to have everything set up before you do the tub because you must **NEVER** leave your child unattended in or near the bathtub, even for one moment. Don't take your eyes away from baby ever because it only takes a moment for a tragedy to happen. So, once you're set up, put on some fun music, get a couple floating bath toys, or even add a few stacking cups for pouring fun. While securely holding your child, help him or her learn to play with the new toys as you soak and enjoy your time together.

30. Give A Massage

Do you find massages relaxing? You might not be so surprised to hear that your baby does too! According to well-known Dr. Sears, "research has shown that baby massage can help babies grow better and behave better… (and the) skin-to-skin connection helps parents and baby better communicate too."[5] Dr. Sears recommends that you start by choosing a comfortable place, look your baby in the eye, bicycle his or her legs gently while telling baby "Relax, relax." Then "cover your baby in an edible oil, such as almond or avocado" (check with your doctor first). "Roll the arms and legs between your hands, and press your thumbs gently into his body. Finish with light strokes to the legs. Slide both hands along the rib cage from center to sides and back again, like flattening the page in a book." There are many books and even some free classes you can take on proper baby massage techniques, which I definitely recommend. Until then, go slowly and be extra gentle.

31. Give a Manicure

It may not be the most fun you'll ever have with your child, but babies' nails eventually become harder (soon after birth they can just be easily torn and don't need clipping), and will need to be cut. The two tools I recommend for this are (1) baby nail scissors, which seem to be MUCH safer than the clippers, and (2) a distraction for your baby. You can try a mobile of some kind, or even your spouse. My husband dances and spins around while chatting non-stop and that seems to mesmerize our son long enough for me to clip his nails. Find what works for you!

---

[5] http://www.parenting.com/article/how-to-massage-your-baby?page=0,0

32. Take Baby's Nose On A Kitchen Tour

There was little my niece and nephew loved to do more than tour my mom's spice rack and tea cupboards. They loved the sights and smells, and began recognizing their favorite bottles right away that they would want her to open and hold close to them. The trick here is to bring bottles close enough to be smelled without getting anything onto your baby or in his or her eyes, nose, or mouth. Some good scents to showcase might be vanilla, cinnamon, chocolate, cumin, clove, rosemary, thyme, sage, curry, and garlic.

33. Kissy Monster

As a parent of a particularly chubby cheeked baby, I just can't get enough of kissing his juicy little face. This is a game of anticipation and physical touch where you "threaten" your baby with the words "I'm gonna get you!" and come at him or her with tickling fingers and cheek kisses aplenty while telling baby, "Oh – I got you!" You can also try feet kisses or blowing raspberries on tummies and feet, which also usually ends up in shrieks of enjoyment (from everyone involved).

34. This Little Piggy (Fingers And Toes)

A fun, portable game to play with your baby that nearly every one of us experienced growing up. Going from largest toe (or thumb, if you're doing this on the hands) to smallest, label each one with the following, "This little piggy went to market" then continue to the next toe, and so on for each, "This little piggy stayed home."

"This little piggy had roast beef." "This little piggy had none (sad face)." "And *this* little piggy went 'wee wee wee wee' all the way home!" Great for clipping nails, drying hands and feet, or general short distractions!

35. SuperBaby

Little kids love playing superhero, and that love starts when they are very young! Once your baby can hold his or her head up securely, a new world of flying possibilities opens up to him or her. Baby can become a superhero, flying about to save the world from general chaos and disaster, a rocketship flying to the moon, a jet taking the President of the USA to an important meeting, or anything else you can imagine.

36. Hola, Amor Mio

Many parents love the idea of starting babies on new languages early. If that's something you're interested in, go for it! This is especially easily accomplished if you speak the other language yourself. Try to take an hour each day to speak to your child in the other language. Get him or her used to the other sounds. Pick up common objects and label them with their alternate names. It's great practice for you and great exposure for your baby.

37. Leader Of The Band

This is a game your baby may start on his or her own without even needing to be introduced to it by you. Once your baby starts more reliably gripping objects you're ready to suit baby up as a one-man band! Setting him up in a safe play place, provide him or her with wooden or plastic spoons, pots, pans, Tupperware, metal bowls, and the like and let baby go to town.

38. Master Of All He/She Surveys

As your baby gains strength and confidence, give him or her opportunities to be "in control" of various things. For example, hold your baby up so he or she can reach and then let your baby turn the lights on and off, open or close the garage door as you leave the house, or hold a little flashlight and see and explore what's around in a dark room. My grandparents even had a special drawer in the kitchen that was filled with safe toys for us (at a height we could get to on our own) and your baby will love having a go-to place for accessing things it's okay to play with. (Just supervise baby with the drawer to avoid a pinch or other finger/body injuries.)

39. Obstacle Course

As your baby gets closer to moving about on his or her own, you'll start to see some pretty impressive acrobatics as baby works to get where he or she wants to go. You can make this a game by setting up a little obstacle course of pillows, cushions, blankets, and laundry baskets. If your baby encounters one that is too tough, help him or her move it aside to avoid baby getting too frustrated to want to continue.

40. Follow The Bouncing Ball

Get a variety of balls (whiffle, foam, plastic, tennis, and rubber with lots of holes) and let your baby experiment. Toss them, drop them, bounce them, put them in buckets, take them out, and roll them. Once he or she can sit up, try rolling them back and forth to each other. This is a game that will be fun for months as you see your baby's skills change and improve.

41. Get It Juuuuuust Right

There's a reason why stacking cups and rings (and measuring cups!) are such popular baby toys. Babies love stacking and arranging different objects, and pouring things from one object to the other (or just onto the ground). If you don't have the store-bought items, you can still have fun by using nesting objects you *do* have around your house. This can be played on the ground or in the bathtub for loads of fun.

42. Can You Get Your Toy?

You can "test" your baby in fun ways by "hiding" his or her toys under Tupperware on the floor. Use clear or translucent Tupperware so that your baby can still actually see the toy despite the plastic barrier between them. Your baby might even discover that the Tupperware becomes the new favorite toy instead of the objects clustered beneath!

43. Mobius Enjoyment

It's almost like circuit training, but once your baby can cruise around you can put together a little loop of endless enjoyment for your baby by creating a variety of stations that flow one to the next. Put a favorite toy on the couch, then the next on the end table, then on the footstool, and back around onto the couch and watch your baby cruise along the little circuit you've created!

Chapter 3: Outdoor (Or Out And About) Activities

44. Blow Bubbles

Many babies are just *mesmerized* by bubbles. You can find bubbles in almost any baby store (or online) and they are often very low cost for the number of hours of entertainment they will provide. Just make sure you're using kid-safe bubble formula (and don't let your kids get the stuff in their mouths anyway). Start out by blowing bubbles and watching your baby track them as they float away.

45. Spray Park or Wading Pools

Most neighborhoods have some kind of little spray park or wading pools nearby for when the weather heats up a bit. These are usually "free" (paid for by your taxes), run by the City, and the water has some chemicals added (like swimming pools do) to keep kids safer who are ingesting it. They often have gentle slopes, are never more than a few inches deep, and offer a fun place for those just learning how to walk to literally "get their feet wet."

46. Urban Safari

If you have pet stores or animal shelters in your area, then you already have little free mini-zoos just awaiting you. Take your little one to see some cats and dogs (but don't get too close, as they may bite or scratch) sleeping, playing, or chasing string. Go to an aquarium shop to see a whole variety of fishes swimming (totally mesmerizing) in dozens of tanks, turtles, and often birds, gerbils and more! Talk to your baby about everything you're seeing, label the animals, and share the different sounds they make (although your baby will probably be hearing all the noises just fine)!

47. Picnic Lunch

It's so important to get out of the house every now and then, and if you're especially busy, combining this with lunch time can be great double duty. Prepare during a nap (if you can) by fixing some tasty nibbles, packing a blanket, sunscreen, hand wipes, and the diaper bag and head out to a nearby park. Let your baby feel the grass, plants, dirt, and sand (this is where the wipes come in handy). Let your baby lie on the blanket and look up at the leaves of trees or clouds passing by. (Don't spend too long in direct sun, as baby's skin is VERY delicate!)

48. Visit The Library

Libraries are great stops because they are usually filled with built-in entertainment: lots of books and lots of kids. People watch and read to your little one, and make sure you stop to find out about their (free) offerings for kids like story time for babies!

49. Make An Action Movie

You may have taken a million photos of your baby, but many parents miss out on taking video. Nowadays most phones have the ability to take video, and some video cameras as very reasonably priced (well under $100 for images that can be uploaded right onto your computer). Think up a little plot starring your baby (baby saves the day from the evil Count Spatula, or the like) and put a couple scenes together. Use your computer's free movie software (which almost all operating systems now come with) splice them together and you'll have some great entertainment for your friends and family, and a video your child will love to see once he is older.

50. Swings At The Park

Find a nearby park that features swings (specifically baby swings) and once your baby is big and strong enough (check with doctor) take him or her out for his first swing. Make sure you bring the camera or video recorder, because you're going to want to capture this on film!

51. Trip To The Zoo

When your baby is old enough for up to 3 hours of entertainment without having to be home for a nap, you're probably ready for a trip to the zoo! See if there's a good one nearby (or aquariums work great too) and see if they have special days or rates when admission is reduced. Your baby may only be up for a couple exhibits his or her first time, so keep your expectations realistic. Consider an annual pass, as many often pay for themselves after only two visits.

52. Texture Trip

Take your baby out for a texture trip by visiting a local craft store. Your baby will love to feel everything he or she can get those little hands on. From yarn, felt, fleece, to cotton, the craft store will be a feast for baby's senses!

53. Walk and Talk

Getting outside and walking around is one of the best natural mood boosters you'll find. Grab your stroller or a carrier (whatever is right for you and your baby) and find a friend who will walk with you, even if just once a month. With just a few such friends, you'll be assured of at least one outing a week with other adults, and time to catch up and stay connected with people who matter in your life.

54. Art Walk/Museum

Most museums have a free day every month (e.g. the first Tuesday of the month, the second Monday of the month). Look up your favorite museums around your city and you're sure to find at least one a week you can visit. Many have rotating exhibits and displays and getting out to see them will not only be good for you, but also fun for your baby. You can even invite other friends (with children or not) to join you and get in some fabulous adult conversations.

55. Nature Walk

Get outside for a nature walk with your baby. Breathe in the fresh air, hug a tree, and let your baby commune with nature (from a safe distance). You can let your baby smell a pine needle, hold little bits of cedar tree, smell a rose, feel a flower petal, and even toss rocks into the water (CLOSELY SUPERVISED – make sure those rocks don't work their way into his or her little mouth!). With enough exposure, you're sure to cultivate your own little nature-lover!

About the Author

Children's author, Christie Cunningham, has a degree in Psychology, studied child and developmental psychology, and worked in an autism center in southern California. She is a mother and loves to create books for children, parents, and caregivers to enjoy that will help families to create lasting positive memories and develop close bonds and attachment.

Cunningham lives in the Pacific Northwest with her family and when she's not busy writing new books she loves playing softball, jogging, spending time outside with her friends, family, niece, and nephews, and getting involved in church and community activities.

33809695R00026

Made in the USA
Lexington, KY
10 July 2014